MOTORCYCLE MAINTENANCE & REPAIR

Text by Calton E. Taylor

Introduction and Photography by Forest H. Belt

THEODORE AUDEL & CO.
a division of
HOWARD W. SAMS & CO., INC.
4300 West 62nd Street
Indianapolis, Indiana 46268

FIRST EDITION

FIRST PRINTING—1974

International Standard Book Number: 0-672-23805-5

Contents

SECTION 3

One-Cylinder Four-Cycle Engines: start with spark plug—gapping it—cleaning older plugs—spark plug reveals engine operating condition—ignition breaker points—condenser—installing new points and condenser—setting the points gap—timing the ignition with a strobe light—the ignition coil—Two-Cylinder Four-Cycle Engines: new spark plug—how to avoid overtightening—replacing entire dual-point breaker assembly (easiest way)—check centrifugal advance weights—replacing points individually—ignition timing procedure, using homemade timing light—time left cylinder first with breaker plate, right cylinder last with rear points—changing condenser—adjusting valve clearance as part of tune-up—Two-Cycle Engine Tune-up: plugs, points, and condenser for single-cylinder engine—same for two-cylinder

SECTION 4

Battery care—fuses—headlights, taillights, and turn flashers

Preface

For several years motorcycles have grown in popularity. They no longer carry the stigma of road gangs and sloppy itinerants. They have, in fact, become an accepted vehicle for family fun and recreation. Motorcycles of all sizes and styles crowd summertime highways.

With gasoline worries that now plague most of the world, the motorcycle seems likely to develop as a personal means of transportation. College professors and mechanics, bookkeepers and bridge builders, workers from every imaginable trade and profession ride motorcycles to and from work. Motorcycles burn so little gasoline, they trim the expense of commuting and may help ease the scarcity (not to mention cutting hydrocarbon pollution).

Owners of motorcycles find most of them dependable. Yet, they also have found that a majority of motorcycles need more attention than an automobile. Motorcycle engines are usually high-performance, even when their size is small. Engines require minor tune-up and adjustment comparatively often. If you know a good motorcycle technician, you're okay. If not, you're on your own. And motorcycles are not much like automobiles; the guy who tinkers with his car could really mess up his motorcycle.

Of course, motorcycle maintenance and minor repairs are not that complicated—anyone handy with tools can learn to perform many small jobs. But there are some facts and features you should know about before you tackle those jobs.

For example, motorcycle engines operate in one of two modes: two-stroke and four-stroke (usually called *two-cycle* and *four-cycle*). They are also classified according to whether they have one cylinder or two. Larger machines have three and four cylinders, but they are in a class of machines not covered in this book. Two-stroke engines have carburetors different from those on four-stroke engines. The ignition system for a two-cylinder does not operate the same as one for a single-cylinder engine. It's these variances you learn about in the pages of this book.

Obviously, not every brand, model, or style of motorcycle can be dealt with in a book this size. Yet the principles involved with the engines and machines shown represent the majority that people buy. Large sport and touring cycles belong in another category, and yet you'll find much of the information of this book applies to them as well. The examples here, however, have been chosen from smaller machines in the 175cc to 350cc range.

You will quickly come to realize, as you study the pages, there are only four significant portions of the machine you can take care of: ignition, carburetion, controls, and electric devices. Because of the overtones of safety, the first section deals with controls and their importance to riding. There, as in all the chapters, the emphasis dwells directly on maintenance, adjustment, and minor repairs.

We hope you find our book valuable. We have taken care that text and photographs be as accurate and revealing as possible. In the course of caring for your own motorcycle, you should save a lot of money on repairs. Your machine will last many years longer than it might otherwise.

FOREST H. BELT

SECTION 1

Service Tips for Safe Riding

No motorcyclist can travel carefree on a bike in poor condition. Regular care and servicing help keep your motorcycle and you safe. This knowledge makes what riding you do more enjoyable.

Most all new motorcycles include a tool kit with enough tools for minor repairs and adjustments. But you can buy equivalent tools for any machine at little cost. For major

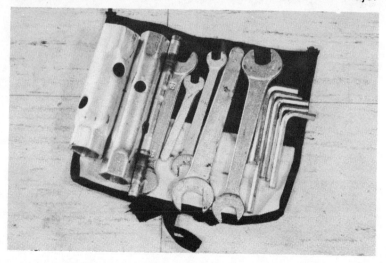

repairs, take your motorcycle to a dealer. Choose a dealer from recommendations of experienced friends. They probably have heard which dealers have the best reputations. A poor service department soon gets found out.

A loose drive chain wears the sprocket teeth and the chain rollers quickly. The rollers wear on the inside when the chain is too tight and stretches so much that the rollers eventually do not match the sprocket teeth.

Once a week, push upward on the bottom of the chain, halfway between the sprockets. The object: to check the chain's tension. Consider one-half inch of movement normal —more or less play denotes need for adjustment. If any adjustment to the chain is needed, or a new chain is to be installed, a center stand must be used to raise the rear wheel off of the ground so it can rotate.

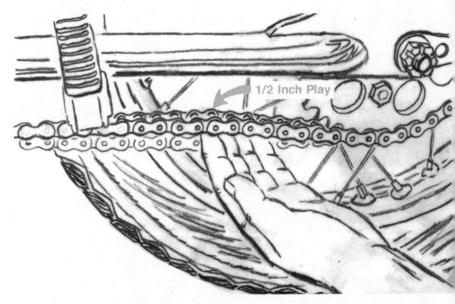

To adjust the chain, you first extract the cotter pin from the rear axle nut. This pin keeps the nut from working loose as you ride. Then loosen the axle nut enough so that the axle slides freely in the lower frame members (called the *swing arms*).

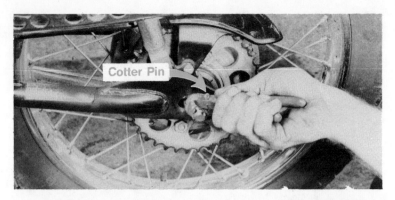

Cotter Pin

Next, loosen the jam nuts on the chain adjuster screws. These nuts keep the screws locked solidly in the yoke part of the adjusters. Now turn the screws on both sides of the wheel, about equally, to reposition the rear wheel. You pull the wheel backward if the chain is loose, forward if too tight. Work the adjusters until you have one-half inch of play in the chain.

There is a series of "hash" marks on the swing arms just above the chain adjuster yokes. Notice how the single mark on each side of each yoke aligns with these marks. This lets you set the marks the same for both adjusters, which keeps the rear wheel rolling straight.

When replacing a bad chain, never take the old one off until you have the new one. Roll the wheel until the master link is along the bottom span of chain. Remove the spring clip from the master link. You will probably have to squeeze

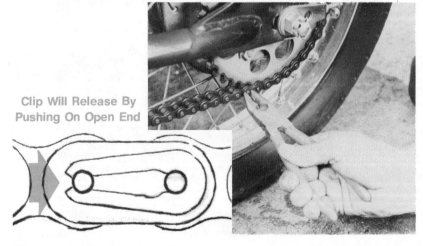

the split end of the clip and the link pin with pliers. Once the split end comes loose from the one pin, you can slide the clip off the other pin by hand. The slot in the clip has a notch wide enough to clear the master link pin.

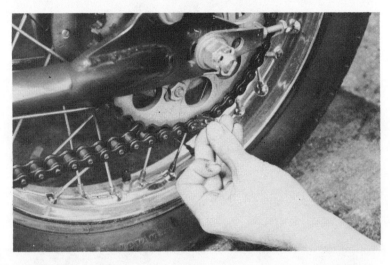

Slide the outside plate off of the master link. The plate should drop off freely.

Having removed the outside plate, push on the master link pins. The pins and inside plate slide out together. To install a new chain, attach the new chain to the old one with

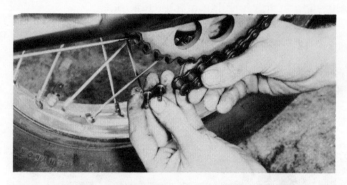

the master link. Use the length of old chain that drapes over the rear sprocket. That leaves the main bottom portion of the old chain free to pull.

Put the gearshift in neutral position—this frees the front drive sprocket so it can rotate. Pull the new chain slowly over the top of the rear sprocket. It thus feeds around the front drive sprocket and back to the rear along the bottom. Stop when the trailing end of the new chain barely rests on the rear sprocket teeth. This simplifies attaching a new master link.

Pull

Unhook the old chain by loosing the old master link. Connect the ends of the new chain together with a new master link. Readjust the chain tension as described previously—oil the chain (if needed) and you have the job completed. Always recheck the rear brakes when you alter the chain adjustment in any way. The procedure is described later in this chapter.

Not every motorcycle owner knows how to remove the rear wheel, but it's important. Changing a rear tire demands the removal of the wheel. You should know *all* of the steps which include more than just pulling a wheel.

First raise the rear wheel. Find the master link and take the drive chain apart as described earlier. This time take both ends of the chain off the rear sprocket. Drop a paper or clean cloth under the chain so it stays clean and out of the dirt.

Next remove the cotter pin from the rear-wheel axle nut. With a wrench, take the axle nut completely off. Use a wrench with a long handle, because this nut should be very tight.

Loosen the jam nut on the chain adjusters. Back the adjuster screws off until each yoke swings down free. Be sure you loosen both sides, or the axle will not slide out.

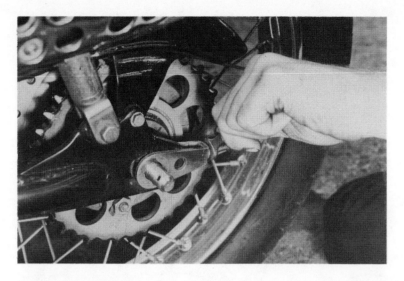

Drive the axle out of the wheel with a rubber mallet. If you have no rubber mallet, replace the nut just far enough that it is flush with the end of the axle. Then you can use a center punch and a steel hammer. The nut protects the threads at the end of the axle rod. Hit the axle with sharp taps instead of crushing blows.

Tap

Rubber Hammer

Now pull the axle shaft all the way out of the wheel (toward the right side on most motorcycles). You will notice a hole in the head of most axles. Place a screwdriver through this hole to form a handle which you can use to remove the axle.

Pull

Slide the rear wheel backward until the axle spacer drops out. You will likely have to pull the brake assembly sideways until it clears the hub before you can roll the wheel out. Now you can go ahead with whatever work you have on the tire or wheel. This rear wheel removal applies only to off-road bikes. When removing rear wheels on street-bikes the brake control assembly must be removed—otherwise the wheel will not clear the fender.

To reinstall the wheel, reverse the procedure just mentioned. Clear the brake shoes inside the hub drum. Roll the wheel forward until you can slide the spacer and axle in place. Thread the right-side chain adjuster yoke onto the axle rod.

Pull

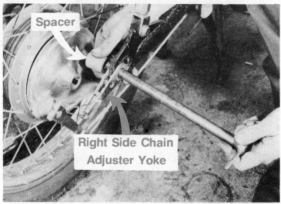

Spacer

Right Side Chain
Adjuster Yoke

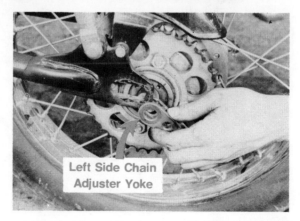

Left Side Chain
Adjuster Yoke

Push or tap the axle through the hub. Hold the left chain adjuster yoke in place, and tap the axle through it. Reinstall the drive chain. Screw the axle nut back on. Leave the axle nut and adjuster nuts loose so you can adjust the chain.

Adjust the chain as described earlier. Match up the alignment marks on both sides very carefully. These marks must be matched exactly, or the rear wheel will not run straight. When you get chain tension just right, set the axle nut as tight as possible with the long-handle wrench. Replace the cotter pin.

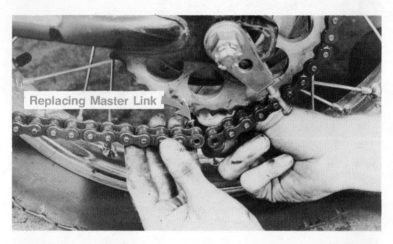

Replacing Master Link

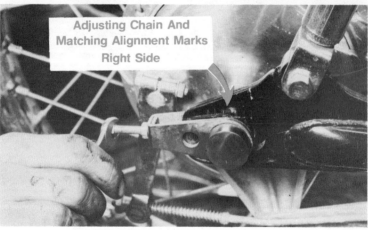

Adjusting Chain And Matching Alignment Marks Right Side

You must always readjust the rear brake, every time the rear wheel has been moved. It is generally easy to adjust. You merely turn the nut on the end of the brake linkage rod. Set it so the brake pedal moves downward a half-inch before the shoes rub the brake drum. Try the pedal up and down with one hand and twist the nut with other. This way you see how much turning the nut needs while you are doing the adjusting.

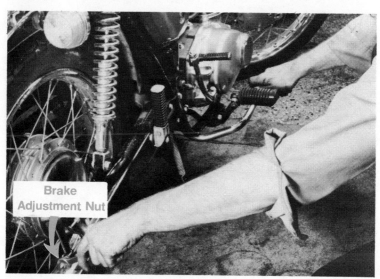

Brake
Adjustment Nut

19

Some motorcycles have a stopscrew to adjust "toe height" on the rear-brake pedal. Turning it changes the topmost or resting position of the pedal for an individual rider's preference. Set the stopscrew so you do not have to rock your foot back on the footrest to reach the brake pedal. You set it only once—immediately after purchasing the motorcycle. It stays the same through all subsequent brake adjustments.

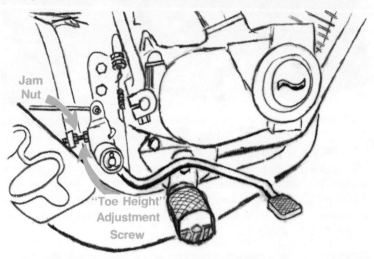

Jam Nut

"Toe Height" Adjustment Screw

After you are sure pedal height is correct, turn the nut on the back end of the linkage rod to adjust the brake-pedal travel. You want one-half inch of pedal movement before the brake shoes touch the drum (which stops the machine).

Brake Adjustment Nut

On a few motorcycle models, instead of a linkage rod, a cable operates the rear brake. For these models, you determine pedal height with a nut at the bracket that secures the front end of the brake cable.

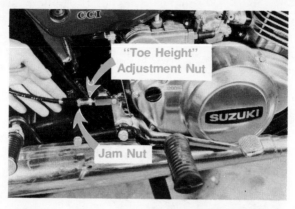

A sleeve with a hexagon-shaped end on it screws into the bracket on the frame. For adjustment, loosen the jam nut and turn the sleeve to reposition the pedal height. Then retighten the jam nut.

Brake adjustment itself resembles those with a linkage rod. A long screw has been welded to the end of the cable nearest the wheel. The screw threads into a lug on the end of a braking arm outside the brake-shoe cover plate. The nut on this screw adjusts the extent of brake-pedal travel.

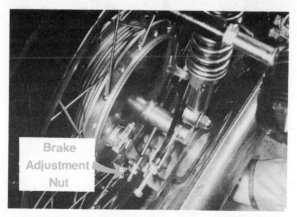

Check the brake-light switch any time you have adjusted the brake. Sometimes you will find it necessary to reposition the switch, to keep the brake light working at proper pedal travel or pressure.

Two of the more popular styles of brake-light switches are *spring-pull* and *button.* The spring-pull unit mounts either above the brake pedal or behind it. A light spring connects pedal to switch, and maneuvers the contact plunger of the switch when you depress the pedal. For adjustment, you loosen the two nuts on the switch barrel; reposition the switch by turning both nuts; then tighten both nuts so the switch fits solidly in the bracket.

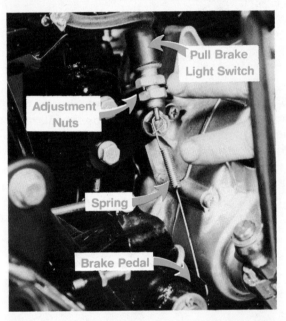

The button-type switch mounts on the swing arm forward of the rear wheel hub. A collar with a tab clamps to the brake linkage rod which moves with it. You adjust the collar so the tab holds the switch button *in* whenever the rider has released the brake pedal. The tab should let the button *out* just enough to turn the brake lights on when the pedal moves about a half-inch downward.

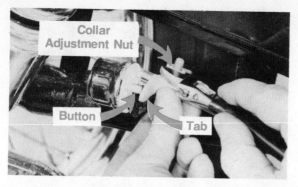

The front-wheel brake lever mounts on the right handle-bar. A cable runs from the hand-lever to a brake arm on the front wheel. You would be well advised to take your motorcycle to a dealer for this adjustment. A slight error could make the front wheel lock up whenever the brake is applied. That's an almost sure invitation to an accident and spill. A locked front wheel tips you over easily. Whenever you need the front brake, always pull the lever *after* you have good pressure on the rear brake. Pull the lever gently until you feel the brake working.

Certain newer motorcycles have a hydraulic front brake. A reservoir to hold brake fluid mounts on the right handle-bar. The hand lever operates a small piston in the bottom of the reservoir. The piston forces brake fluid down a steel

tubing to cylinders at the front wheel. Fluid pressure in the cylinders applies the brake.

Check the fluid level once a month. Whenever you add fluid to the reservoir, you may also have to bleed the brake system to remove any air that gets into the tubing. You will find the bleeder plug on top of the wheel cylinder, directly below where the tubing attaches. Loosen the bleeder plug slightly while you squeeze the brake lever. This forces any air in the line down to the wheel cylinder, and out the bleeder plug. Squeeze until the sputtering around the plug stops and

only fluid seeps out. Tighten the bleeder plug before you release the lever. That prevents more air from entering the system.

Once a steady stream of fluid seeps out of the bleeder plug, top off the brake-fluid level in the reservoir. Finally, tighen the cap securely.

The clutch lever mounts on the left handlebar. A cable runs from the lever on the handlebar to a clutch lever or arm on the side of the transmission. Lubricate this cable at least twice every summer. If you ride the motorcycle in dusty areas, lubricate the cable once a month.

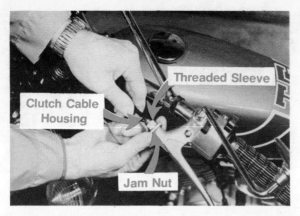

Clutch Cable Housing

Threaded Sleeve

Jam Nut

The clutch-cable housing fits into a threaded sleeve at the handlebar lever. The sleeve in turn screws into the front of the lever bracket. This sleeve adjusts how much free play the cable allows the hand lever. Loosen the circular jam nut and screw the sleeve almost all the way in. Then align the slots in the sleeve and the jam nut with the slot in the lever bracket.

Hold the cable housing with one hand and squeeze the lever tightly with the other. Then, as you release the lever, pull the cable and housing away from the bracket and slide the cable out of the slots. This frees the cable from its bracket.

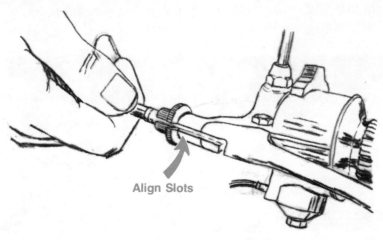

Align Slots

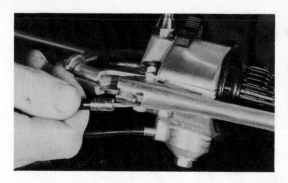
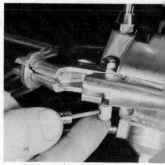

Flip the slug on the end of the cable out of the notch in the hand lever. Use dry powdered-graphite lubricant. You can buy it from most dealers, and from bearing suppliers. The newest version comes in an aerosol can with a small plastic tube at the nozzle. Push the little tube down into the cable housing alongside the cable and spray. Later, as you operate the clutch lever, the lubricant works its way down the entire cable.

Restoring the cable to the hand lever takes a little manipulation. First push the slug back into its notch in the lever. Next, tug on the cable housing with one hand, baring enough of the cable to slide into the slots in the lever, sleeve, bracket, and jam nut. The pull is heavy and it is hard to hold the cable housing in that position. So rest the end of the cable housing on the jam nut. The jam nut makes a temporary stop for the cable housing.

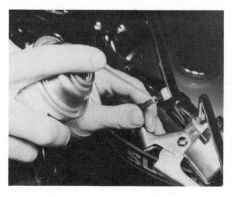

Then you squeeze the lever with your other hand (usually the left) to pull the cable as far out of the housing as possible. This provides enough distance between cable housing and slug that the cable can drop into the slots with the sleeve impeding the housing.

As you release the hand-lever, pressure pulls the cable housing backward with the cable until the housing slips over the end of the sleeve. Let the end of the cable housing ease down into the hole in the sleeve.

You are now ready to adjust the cable. Screw the sleeve out (counterclockwise) until you have taken all the slack out of the cable. Operate the clutch lever a few times to assure that the cable does not bind. Screw the sleeve inward enough to leave a free-play gap of ⅛ inch between the lever tip and the bracket.

Tighten the jam nut against the bracket to lock the adjustment sleeve. If the slots all happen to line up, turn the sleeve and jam nut just enough to separate the slots.

Rest Cable Housing On Jam Nut

Pulling Cable From Housing
Squeeze

Pull While Releasing Lever

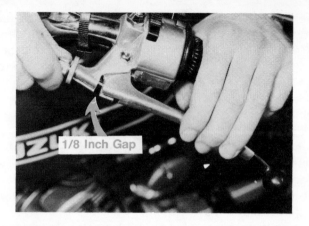

1/8 Inch Gap

A twist-grip on the right handlebar operates as throttle control. A cable pulled by the twist-grip moves a slide in the carburetor. As the slide moves upward, the fuel intake opening to the engine increases in size. This allows more air/fuel vapor into the engine, and the engine runs faster.

A hollow screw and sleeve on the cable housing directly below the twist-grip provide a way to adjust play in the throttle cable. First loosen the jam nut on the sleeve. Then turn the screw just enough to allow ⅛ inch of free play between the cable housing and the sleeve. Retighten the jam nut.

Most motorcycle tachometers operate from a cable driven by a gear from the camshaft. The tachometer indicates the revolutions per minute (rpm) of the engine crankshaft. The reading on the tachometer shows double the rpm, at which

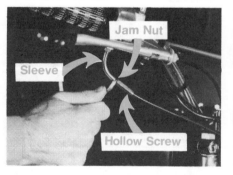

Jam Nut

Sleeve

Hollow Screw

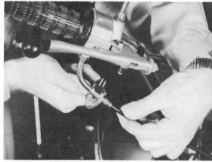

the camshaft turns, since the camshaft goes around once for each two revolutions of the crankshaft. Hence the 2:1 drive gear.

You need to lubricate this cable once a year (normal riding conditions). Or, if you notice the tachometer needle "bouncing" while the engine runs steadily, the cable probably needs lubricant.

Unscrew the nut on the cable drive unit. Lift the cable housing up clear of the drive unit. Then pull the cable downward, part-way out of the housing. Spray the cable with the same lubricant you use on the clutch cable. Reinstall the cable. Tighten the cable nut well at the engine housing.

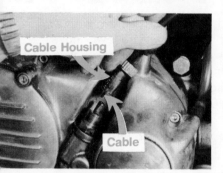
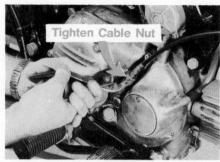

Two-cycle engines for motorcycles come equipped with an oil injection device. A pump drives oil through a tiny jet into the carburetor, where the spray of oil mixes with the fuel vapor going to the cylinders. Separate oil lines to both ends of the crankshaft supply oil to all the bearings that support the chankshaft. The oil mixed with the gasoline lubricates only the piston and rings.

A small tank holds the oil for this system. Put only two-cycle engine oil in this tank. The throttle cable connects to, and operates, the injection pump as you open the throttle, meeting the varying lubrication needs of the engine. Snapping a rubber plug out of the oil-pump cover exposes the cable adjustment. Notice the alignment marks on the pump lever and on the housing. With the throttle closed (at idling position), the mark on the lever should match the one on the housing.

Marks Align
At Idle Position

If the marks do not align, twist the throttle a few times to assure that nothing sticks or binds when the lever moves. If nothing sticks and the marks still do not match, loosen the cable jam nut on the side of the pump housing and screw cable in or out until marks align. With marks aligned, tighten jam nut and twist the throttle a few times to recheck your adjustment. The pump cover is removed only to show interior construction—but does not have to be removed for adjustment.

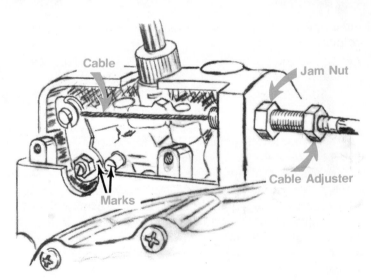

Cable

Jam Nut

Cable Adjuster

Marks

Always check the oil level in a four-cycle engine before you start. Make a habit of this, so you never run the engine without oil. Change oil at least every 1000 miles. If you ride your motorcycle in a dusty area, change the oil more often. Use only a good grade of oil recommended by the manufacturer.

Removing Plug To Check Oil Level

Oil Level Should Be To This Mark

Some motorcycles use a separate tank for larger oil capacity. A pump circulates the tank oil through the engine, providing better lubrication than a crankcase reservoir can supply alone.

Mufflers on motorcycle with two-cycle engines contain a removable baffle tube. Two screws at the rear of the muffler hold the baffle tube inside the muffler. Remove the baffle

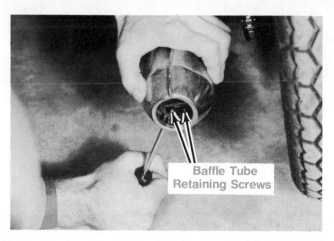

Baffle Tube Retaining Screws

Baffle Tube

tubes and clean them every two months. If the oil injection unit runs too much oil, you'll probably have to clean the baffle tubes when you adjust the oil injection. Scrape the outside of the baffle tube with a putty knife. After scraping, wash the tube with gasoline for a final cleansing.

Fuel System

We will start off this chapter by mentioning a common winter-storage problem with motorcycles. Gasoline tends to "break up" if left in the tank all winter. Yet, an empty tank rusts easily.

An additive like *Sta-Bil* solves these problems with gasoline. It stabilizes the gas and prevents gum deposits in the carburetor. Most motorcycle dealers carry it. You add a can to the gas tank just before storage time. Run the engine long enough that *Sta-Bil* treated gas gets into the carburetor. Then fill up the fuel tank with gasoline. That way, no rust can form inside from condensation.

The fuel system described here is typical of that on one-cylinder two-cycle engines. Start all such servicing with the air cleaner. One nut holds the outer cover on. Remove this cover to gain access to the filter.

Notice the rubber washer in the center. Do not lose this washer. It keeps the cover from rattling or vibrating loose when the engine is running. It also retains the filter, in case the cover should loosen.

Air Cleaner Outer Cover

Rubber Washer

Slide the filter out of the housing. Wash foam-rubber filters in clean gasoline. After washing, soak the foam-rubber element with motor oil. Oil in the tiny pockets of the foam rubber traps dust particles in the air keeping them from entering the carburetor. Wash the filter every two months during riding season. If you ride in dusty areas, do it every month.

Before you replace the filter, wipe out the inside of the air cleaner housing. This removes any dirt that has fallen off of the filter when you removed it.

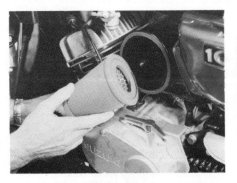

Remove the tiny sediment bowl which screws into the bottom of the fuel shutoff valve. You may have to loosen the bowl with a wrench, but you can always remove it by hand. This prevents damage to the threads. Use the same care replacing it, using a wrench only to tighten slightly after the bowl is firmly screwed in.

Look in the bowl for dirt or rust from the gas tank. You can usually see any particles gathered in the bottom of the bowl. Remove and flush out the sediment bowl once every month. You will also know whether you're buying clean gasoline.

Wipe out the sediment bowl thoroughly with a clean cloth. This removes any particles stuck to the bottom of the bowl. While the bowl is off, you should verify fuel flow from the tank. Hold the sediment bowl under where it fits and turn the shutoff valve on. Do not let the gas running out of the

Loosen Or Tighten Slightly With Wrench

Remove And Replace Bowl By Hand

Check Bowl For Dirt Or Rust

Checking Fuel Flow

valve splatter on the motorcycle—if it does, wipe it off quickly, as it mars the paint.

Now for some carburetor essentials. Styles vary, but most are similar in many respects. These pages reveal those similarities enough that you can figure out the variances. Remove the side cover to gain access to the carburetor on this small motorcycle. Not all brands of motorcycles have this mounting, even though many use this type of carburetor. The cover protects the carburetor when you ride the motorcycle in rough country off the road.

You will see the drain plug for the float bowl in the lower corner of the carburetor. You can remove this plug to deter-

Removing Carburetor
Side Cover

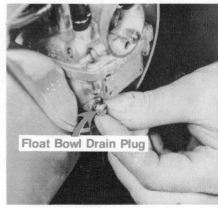

Float Bowl Drain Plug

mine if fuel flows into the carburetor normally. With the plug out, turn the fuel valve on. If the fuel lines and ports into the carburetor are clear, gasoline runs out of the drain hole almost immediately. Before you replace the plug, be sure the tiny gasket is not broken or mashed.

You will find an air/fuel *mixture* screw just inside the lip of the air intake. This screw controls the air/fuel ratio at idling speed. You can adjust it effectively only with the engine running. You have achieved proper adjustment when the engine idles smoothly, yet accelerates without hesitation when you twist the throttle rapidly.

There is an idling *speed* screw on top of the carburetor, outside, right beside the throttle cable. Adjust it whenever

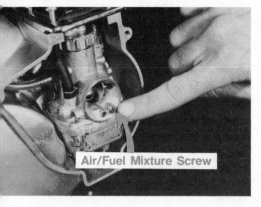

you need to, so the engine idles at 1100 revolutions per minute (rpm).

The next few pages show one fuel system typical in motorcycles with a two-cylinder two-cycle engine. Fuel shutoff, with the valve you see here, works automatically. Vacuum from the engine moves a diaphragm inside the flat housing on the side of the valve. This diaphragm opens the valve only when the engine is running, and gas can run down to the carbs.

This arrangement lets you know immediately if a carburetor leaks the fuel out of the float bowl overnight. The engine can not start the next morning unless the float bowl stays full. No start, no vacuum, no fuel flow. So, what can you do?

This type of valve has no OFF position since the diaphragm shuts off the fuel flow when you shut the engine down. But

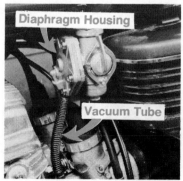

notice the PRI (prime) position. It opens the valve to bypass the diaphragm-controlled action. Use this position only when the engine will not start at the ON position. If the engine regularly will not start after sitting awhile, unless you turn the valve to the PRI position, the carburetors probably leak.

Turn the valve to the RES (reserve) position if you happen to run out of gas. This releases enough extra gasoline to get you to a filling station. Do not try to stretch it far, though; the reserve corner of the tank offers only a few extra miles.

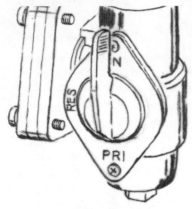

Prime Position

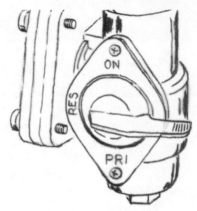

Reserve Position

You can adjust the air/fuel idling mixture with a screw that faces outward, about halfway down on the carburetor. With two carburetors, you must move this screw the same on both. Adjust them only with the engine running at idle speed. Set them so the engine idles smoothly and accelerates evenly and without hesitation.

Air/Fuel
Idling Screw
Left Side

Air/Fuel
Idling Screw
Right Side

The carburetor drain plug is situated at the extreme bottom of the float bowl. Unscrew this plug to verify that fuel enters the carburetor. With the plug out, twist the fuel shut-off valve handle to the PRI position. A stream of gasoline runs out of the drain hole almost immediately when the fuel paths are clear. If no gas runs out, expect to find a plugged or pinched fuel line or some sediment blocking the shutoff valve.

A rubber "boot" covers the tops of both carburetors. Pry the boot out of its mounting groove and slip it up on the throttle cable, out of the way. That gives you access to the idle-speed adjusting screw.

Carburetor Drain Plug Removed

The screws on both carburetors must end up delivering the same amount of fuel to each of the two cylinders. Adjust the idle speed to keep the engine idling smoothly at 1500 revolutions per minute (rpm). Before you replace the rubber boot, rub a light film of oil on the bottom of it. The rubber rim then slides into the mounting groove easier.

Idle Speed Adjusting Screw

Now let's examine the fuel system typical of a single-cylinder four-cycle engine for motorcycles. This carburetor has a primer instead of a choke butterfly.

Before you try starting a cold engine, depress the priming lever for a few seconds. This forces the float down, and the float chamber overflows. The excess fuel runs into the air intake passage. Even a small amount of extra fuel mixing with the air puts a richer vapor mixture into the cylinder and makes starting a cold engine easier. DO NOT "pump" the primer or you can damage the needle valve operated by the float.

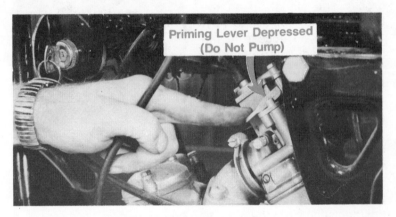

Priming Lever Depressed
(Do Not Pump)

A small fuel filter on this carburetor does the job of a sediment bowl. You will find the filter behind a covered angle fitting at the carburetor end of the fuel line. You may have to hold the tachometer cable out of the way with one hand as you remove the center screw that holds the cover.

Pull the fitting back away from the carburetor. You can then lift the filter out of the carburetor. Inspect it carefully for sediment. Replace it whenever you see any dirt. Check the condition of this filter at least once a month during the riding season.

The idling mixture screw sits just above the float bowl on this carburetor, facing outward to the left side of the motorcycle. Adjust it only with the engine running. As with the others, set it so the engine idles smoothly, yet accelerates evenly when you open the throttle.

Removing Filter Cover

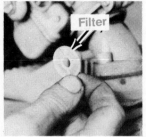

Filter

The idling *speed* screw is on the same side of the carburetor and just above the mixture screw. Set idle speed
for this kind of engine at 900 rpm.

Any time you find it necessary to adjust the carburetor,
particularly the idling speed, take a close look at the throttle cable. It must be seated properly in the top of the carburetor, or you cannot set the idle speed properly. Also
verify that the throttle-grip "play" has not been misadjusted.

Air/Filter
Idle Screw

Idle Speed Screw

Throttle Cable Housing
Must Be Seated
With 1/8 Inch Play

Here is a carburetor used only by *Harley-Davidson,* on
models with two-cylinder four-cycle engines. It's a side-draft
venturi-type carburetor.

Two Phillips screws hold the air cleaner cover. Lift out
the dry-paper filter. Hold it up to a light, and replace it
when no light shines through. A dirty filter does not allow
enough air to enter the carburetor; the engine cannot run
properly, and uses too much gasoline.

Remove the air cleaner backing plate for access to the
carburetor. When you remove the three Phillips screws take

care not to damage the gasket between backing plate and carburetor. It keeps unfiltered air from leaking into the carburetor. One bolt holds a brace behind the plate. Remove it and the backing plate can be removed.

Dry-Paper Filter

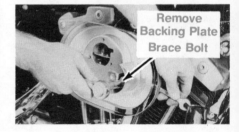

Remove Backing Plate Brace Bolt

The choke knob on this machine mounts directly behind the carburetor on the opposite side of the engine. A cable operates the choke butterfly in the carburetor air-intake passage. The cable opens and closes the butterfly to allow more and less air into the carburetor. When the choke closes, a richer fuel-vapor mixture enters the engine, which makes a cold engine easier to start.

The only adjustment for the choke consists of setting the cable to hold the butterfly completely open when you push the knob in. A small screw on the butterfly control arm holds the cable end in place. Loosen this screw. Hold the butterfly completely open and the choke knob pushed in. Retighten the screw. Now the choke butterfly will not restrict air flow.

Choke Knob

Choke Butterfly Adjustment Screw

The carburetor drain plug fits in the bottom of the float bowl. Shut off the fuel supply at the tank before you remove this plug. With the plug out, turn the fuel on. A few seconds later, fuel should run out—if nothing in the fuel system is stopped up.

If no gas runs out the float-bowl drain, turn the fuel valve off again. Remove the fuel line at the shutoff valve. See if fuel flows through the valve. Blow through the fuel line (by mouth) to dislodge any particles of dirt around the float needle. Reattach the fuel line. Repeat until you have a stream of fuel running from the float bowl.

You will see two screws on top of the carburetor. The one nearest the engine adjusts idling mixture. Have the engine running. Turn the screw inward to where the engine almost dies. Then back it out one-and-one-half turns. From

Removing Carburetor Drain Plug

Air/Fuel Idle Screw

there, you can fine-adjust it so the engine idles smoothly and accelerates evenly without hesitation.

The idling *speed* screw works as a stop for the throttle linkage. It is in a small ear on the rear side of the carburetor. Set it so the tachometer reads 900 rpm with the throttle closed.

A small screw clamps the end of the throttle cable to the linkage. Loosen this screw if you need to adjust the top-speed throttle position. Do it with the engine off, of course. Hold the throttle arm on the carburetor in its wide-open position. Then turn the twist-grip all the way toward you. Retighten the screw. That positions the cable properly in relation to the linkage.

Idle Speed Screw

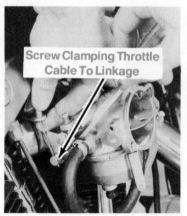

Screw Clamping Throttle Cable To Linkage

Ignition Tune-up

Let's look first at the ignition system of a single-cylinder four-cycle engine. You start any tune-up procedure with the spark plug. A deep-well socket wrench (or the spark-plug socket tool provided in your motorcycle tool kit) reaches deep enough to loosen the spark plug.

Finish removing the plug by hand. This way, you will know if the threads in the engine head have become damaged. If it takes a wrench to back the spark plug all the way out, roll the motorcycle down to your service dealer. He has a tool to restore the threads to good condition. Never try to

Socket Wrench To
Loosen Spark Plug

Once Loosened
Remove Plug By Hand

45

force a new spark plug into damaged threads. This will only ruin the cylinder head, an expensive damage.

Before you install a new spark plug, check its electrode gap with a spark-plug feeler gauge. Set the gap with the .030 wire or blade (that's 30 thousandths of an inch). The gauge should touch both ground and center electrodes lightly. If you decide to reuse the old spark plug, clean both electrodes thoroughly. Then reset the gap to .030 before reinstalling the spark plug in the engine.

The condition of the spark plug reveals much about the engine's operating qualities. Lead deposits on the tip indicate that the plug's heat range is too cold. Your dealer can recommend a slightly hotter spark plug for your machine.

Too Cold
Dark Lead Deposits

When you are using a spark plug with heat range too hot, the electrode burns away quickly. This condition, too, demands attention from your dealer. He knows, by experience, how to judge what range of spark plug you need for your kind of riding.

Too Hot
White Burnt
Appearance

A spark plug covered with deposits of black soot or carbon indicates a too-rich fuel mixture. Changing the main fuel-mixture jet in the carburetor corrects this trouble. But take your motorcycle to a dealer for technical work such as this.

Too Rich
Black Sooty
Appearance

Ignition breaker points come next. They mount on the right side of the engine illustrated here. A small round cover protects the points and keeps them clean. Remove two Phillips screws, and you can pry the cover off with a flat screwdriver.

Be careful not to damage the gasket under the cover. It keeps dirt and oil out of the points compartment. Replace the gasket with a new one if you damage or break it. The

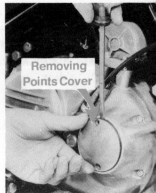

Removing
Points Cover

points burn quickly if dirt, oil, or any matter contaminates the contact faces.

A single screw holds the condenser body in place beside the breaker points. A wire connects the condenser center to the armature portion of the points.

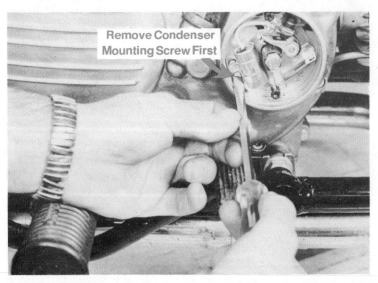

Remove Condenser
Mounting Screw First

Remove the condenser mounting screw first. Then loosen and extract the screws holding the breaker points in place. Points and condenser both can be lifted out of the compartment.

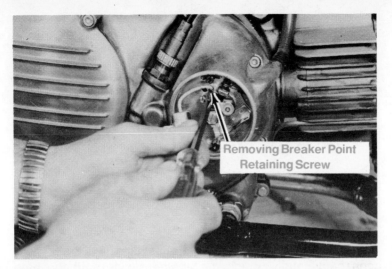

Removing Breaker Point
Retaining Screw

Now you can easily reach the nut that holds the ignition wire to the points armature. Loosen the nut with a small ignition wrench or narrow-tip pliers. The ignition wire terminal in most machines slides off the connector post without having to remove the nut completely.

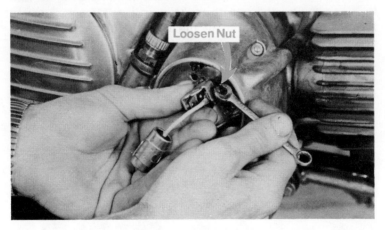

Loosen Nut

Another nut (but sometimes the same nut) on the same connector post holds the primary wire from the ignition coil. Disconnect it. Install new points and condenser by reversing the procedure.

49

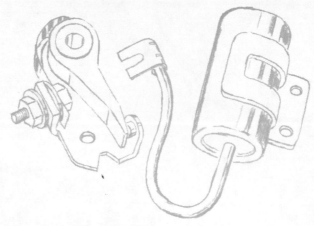

With new condenser and points installed, and both wires connected solidly, crank the engine slowly until the high point on the breaker cam opens the points the widest. Set the points gap with a feeler gauge. Your Owner's Manual lists the proper gap for your model of motorcycle. It varies, according to machine, from 15 to 25 thousandths (.015–.025) of an inch. Crank the engine over a few more times and then remeasure the gap to make sure it's correct. Replace the cover, being mindful of the gasket. It should seal the compartment.

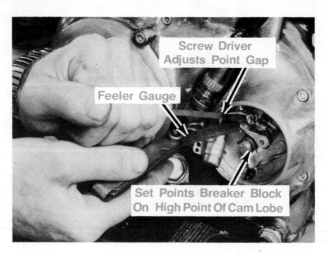

Screw Driver
Adjusts Point Gap

Feeler Gauge

Set Points Breaker Block
On High Point Of Cam Lobe

The wire terminal on some kinds of points uses a clip mounting instead of the machine-screw post. The condenser and coil wires slip into a groove beside the points armature spring. Otherwise, the points and condenser mount as already shown.

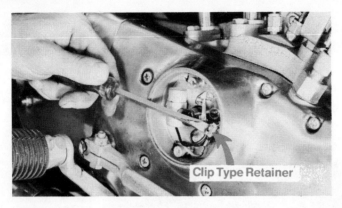

Clip Type Retainer

Ignition *timing* makes the spark plug fire at the proper time during the piston stroke. Use an automotive strobe light. Connect the largest cable of the strobe to the spark plug. You may have to use a small piece of stiff wire to be able to insert the strobe wire between the spark plug and the spark plug wire. Clip the bare wire to the spark plug, using the clamp on the end of the timing-light cable.

The other two wires on the timing light clip to the motor-cycle battery terminals. The ends of the wires are color coded for polarity. BE SURE you get them connected right. Hook the red clip to the positive (+) battery terminal and the black clip to the negative (−) terminal.

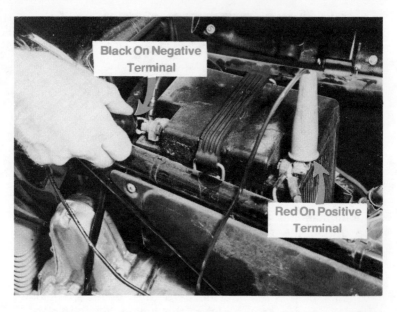

A rubber plug covers the hole in the engine cover where you check timing. Remove the cover with a screwdriver. The proper timing mark on the alternator rotor has a zero (0) beside it. With the engine running, this zero mark must exactly match the pointer mark just above the rotor each time the strobe light comes on.

If the marks do not match, shut the engine off. Crank the engine slowly by hand until these two marks line up. Take off the points cover on the opposite side of the engine. Loosen the breaker plate so it can be rotated gradually until the timing light flashes once.

Retighten the screw and start the engine. The flashes of the strobe light should make the marks appear stopped exactly below the pointer. You know the timing is set correctly.

52

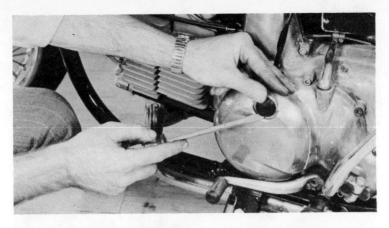

Using Timing Light To
Check Ignition Timing

The ignition coil supplies the high-voltage ignition spark for the spark plug. The coil bolts to the frame directly under the fuel tank on this machine. A small wire on the end runs to the breaker points. The large wire carries spark to the plug.

Testing the ignition coil calls for equipment that only your dealer has. If you know the coil is defective, you can get a new one and make the repair. But coils do not often break down. Let your dealer make sure.

The next several pages explore rather thoroughly the complete tune-up procedure for motorcycles with a two-cylinder four-cycle engine. Some of the repairs shown here apply only to the example chosen, a *Honda* motorcycle. But the principles apply to many.

Replace spark plugs first. Use the socket provided in your tool kit to remove and replace the spark plug. Set the electrode gap on the new plug with a feeler gauge.

When you install the new plug, use a screwdriver for a handle in the socket. Tighten the spark plug only enough to spring the screwdriver blade slightly. This method serves as a simple "torque wrench" and helps you avoid over-tightening the spark plug.

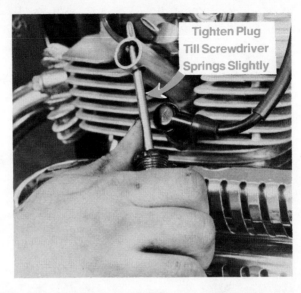

Tighten Plug
Till Screwdriver
Springs Slightly

In this engine, the breaker points mount on the left side near the top. Remove the chrome cover and its gasket for access to the points assemblies.

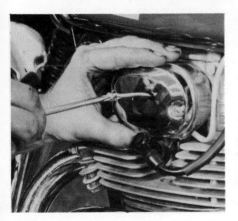

Replacement points are available in two different packagings. You can buy a whole breaker plate assembly with the points already mounted on it. This provides an easy quick method of changing the points. But this way is also more expensive. A pair of screws hold the breaker plate in position. Remove only these screws to release the complete breaker plate assembly.

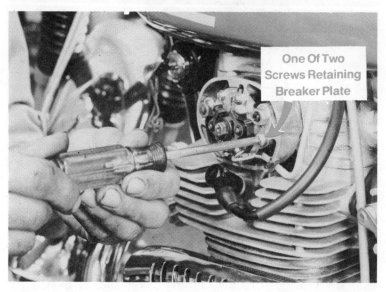

One Of Two
Screws Retaining
Breaker Plate

Before you attempt to remove the breaker plate, it's a good idea to lift the fuel tank up and move it toward the right side. This reveals the wires running from ignition coil to breaker plate. These wires plug together at a connector close to the coil. New breaker plate assemblies come with these wires already in place. You only unplug the old and reattach the new wires when you change the breaker-point plate assembly. Unplug the wires and pull the breaker plate away from the engine.

Before you install the new breaker plate, make a quick check of the centrifugal advance. Grasp the breaker cam with one hand and turn it as far as you can. As the breaker cam turns, the lob weight behind the breaker plate should move slightly. Quick twists of the cam make the lob weights

Lifted
Tank Reveals
Ignition Wires

Unplug
Breaker Plate
Wires

After Unplugging Wires
Breaker Plate Is Pulled

move back and forth. These weights must move freely, or the timing cannot advance properly when you accelerate the engine.

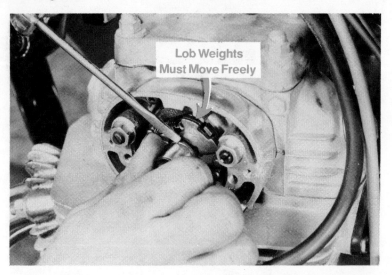

Coat the breaker cam lightly with grease to prevent excessive wear on the points breaker-block. Use only light-viscosity grease or petroleum jelly for the lubricant. Remember, just use a little. Excess grease on the cam flies off onto the contact faces of the points. That causes premature burning.

Now slide the new breaker plate into place. Make sure the two notches on top of the breaker plate line up with the notch in the housing. Center the notches in the plate

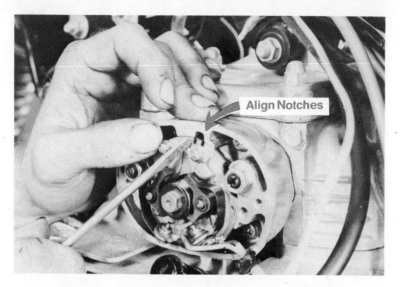

Align Notches

and then snug down the mounting screws slightly. Leave the pressure slack enough that the breaker plate can slide under the screws. You'll be rotating the breaker plate when you set the timing later.

Snug Down
Retaining Screws

As you work the wires of the new breaker assembly into position, see that the rubber grommet on the wires stays in place. The grommet fits down into the slot in the housing where the wire enters the points compartment. This grommet protects the wire insulation from rubbing or chafing. Prolonged rubbing wears the insulation and would short out the ignition system.

Reconnect the wires at the coil and condenser (up under the fuel tank). This completes the breaker plate replacement. But leave the cover off until you have set the points gap and the timing.

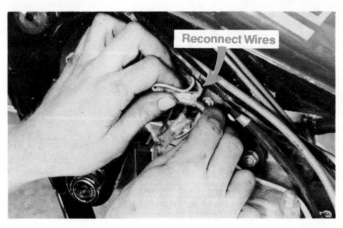

Reconnect Wires

Replacing the points sets individually saves you money. But the amount of work involved may make up the difference. Nevertheless, here's how to proceed with installing points only.

Use a pair of sharp-nose pliers or an ignition wrench to remove the coil and condenser wires from the points. Work with only one set of points at a time. That way, you cannot possibly put the wires on the wrong set of points.

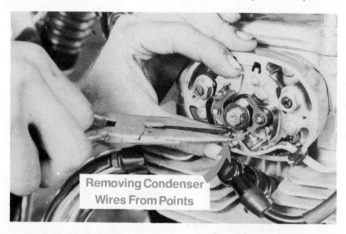

Removing Condenser Wires From Points

Also remember the sequence in which you remove the washers and wire ends from the screw posts. You must replace them all exactly as they came off; otherwise, the connections may be poor.

Remember Sequence Of Wires And Washers

One screw holds the points to the breaker plate. Removing it releases the points for replacement. Before you attempt to install the new points, carefully inspect the old set. The contact faces tell you a lot about the condition of the ignition system. The contact faces should never pit much before 5000 miles. Premature pitting indicates the condenser needs replacing. (Condensers on motorcycles last longer than in automobiles. You do not always replace the condenser with new points.)

Removing Points
Retaining Screw

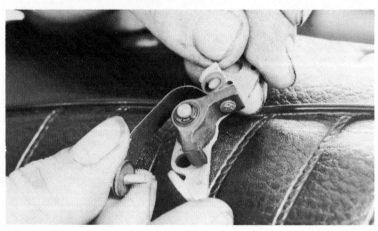

Attach the coil and condenser wires to the new points exactly as they came off the old set. A new terminal screw comes mounted on the points spring. This post holds the wires to the points and also holds the armature spring to the breaker plate.

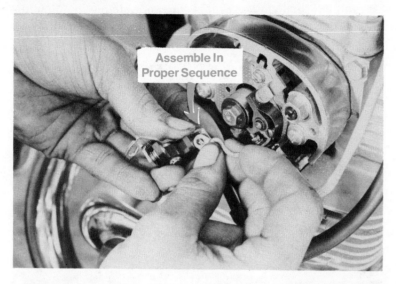

Hold the points in place on the breaker plate and install the mounting screw. Do not try to set the points gap yet. The timing procedure paragraph includes the points gap. Replace the second set of points, using the procedure just described.

Start the ignition-timing sequence by taking off the alternator cover. Sometimes the screws holding the cover have been installed too tight to loosen with a plain Phillips screwdriver. Go to your dealer. He has (or should have) a tool called an *impact driver*. This tool turns the screw backward as you hit its handle with a hammer. Many auto-supply stores carry the impact driver in stock, if you want to buy one; but you will use it rarely.

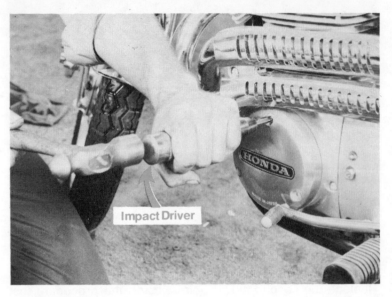

Impact Driver

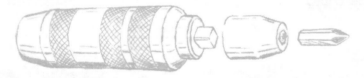

Before removing the cover, set a pan under the engine. A bit of crankcase oil seeps into the alternator case, and runs out when you remove the cover. If very much oil runs out, check the oil level before you start the engine again, and add some if necessary.

Twist the center (rotor) of the alternator until the front points open. A wrench is the easiest way; the whole rotor

Twist Rotor To
Front Point Contact's
Maximum Opening

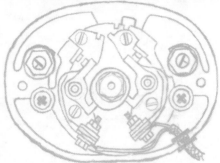

turns, not just the nut. This front breaker set triggers spark for the left cylinder.

With the point contacts spread by the cam to their maximum opening, set the gap with a feeler gauge. Set the points gap on *Honda* two-cylinder engines at .012 to .016 inch. Gaps for other machines are near this value, usually a few thousandths wider.

Gaps must be set whether you replace the complete breaker plate assembly or just the points alone. A notch in the end of the points base offers the means for moving the points (with a screwdriver) for the proper setting.

Begin the timing procedure (for this particular model) by attaching an easily made timing light. The bulb is a small 12-volt lamp in a socket with two wires. You can purchase

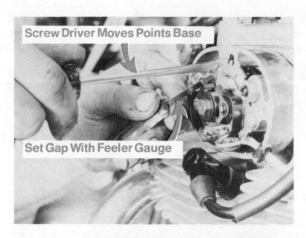

Screw Driver Moves Points Base

Set Gap With Feeler Gauge

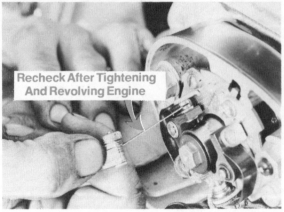

Recheck After Tightening And Revolving Engine

lamp and holder at any auto-supply store or at some hardware stores. Attach an alligator or some other suitable clip to each wire. The mechanic who arranged these pictures used a cotter pin on the ground wire, because it was handy. Attach one wire to the points armature spring and ground the other wire firmly on the engine (here, with the cotter pin).

Through this hookup, primary ignition voltage runs through the points whenever they are closed. But when the points open, the voltage is applied to the bulb and turns it on. Attach the clip to the front set of points first. The initial timing adjustment must be for the left cylinder.

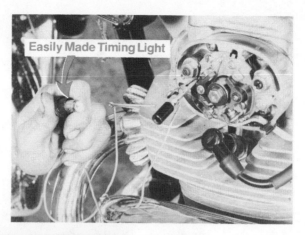

Easily Made Timing Light

Attach Clip To Front Set Of Points First

Letters stamped in the rotor frame in the alternator identify the timing marks. You line these marks up with a mark on the pole piece of the top front (or top left) alternator coil.

Use the mark stamped "LF" to time the left cylinder. Twist the rotor counterclockwise until the "LF" mark aligns. When the rotor reaches this position *exactly*, the front set of points should just start to open. The timing bulb lights.

If timing is incorrect, leave the marks exactly aligned. Rotate the whole breaker plate until the front set of points just starts to open. You'll know, because that's when the light comes on. This procedure correctly sets the timing

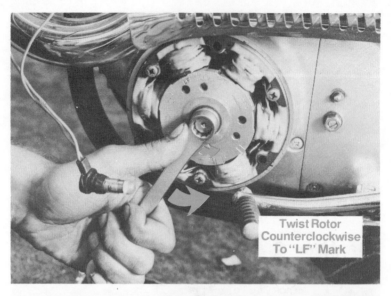

Twist Rotor
Counterclockwise
To "LF" Mark

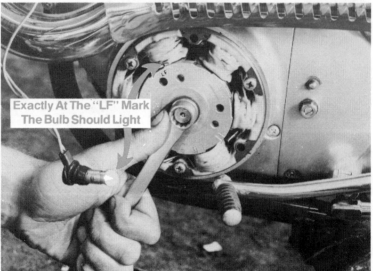

Exactly At The "LF" Mark
The Bulb Should Light

for the left cylinder only. Tighten the breaker plate screws so the plate cannot rotate any further.

Now clip the timing-light wire to the armature spring on the rear set of points. These points trigger the spark to fire

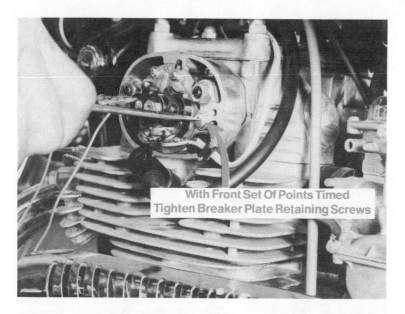

With Front Set Of Points Timed
Tighten Breaker Plate Retaining Screws

the right cylinder. Make sure the clip touches the spring only. The light will not turn on if the clip accidentally grounds to the breaker plate.

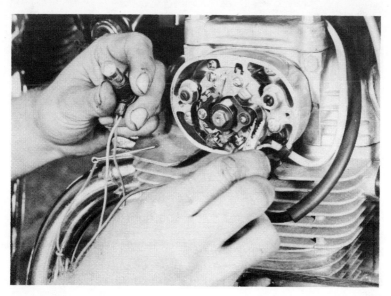

With your wrench, turn the rotor counterclockwise until timing mark "F" lines up with the mark on the top front (or top left) coil. This situates the rotor for the rear set of points. The light may not turn on, however, until you set the rear points gap correctly. When the light *does not* come on as the marks line up, timing is said to be *late*.

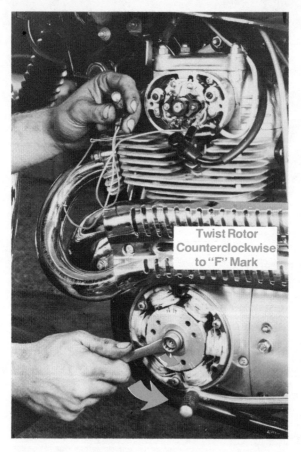

Twist Rotor Counterclockwise to "F" Mark

With the points gap too wide, the light comes on before the timing marks line up (turning the rotor counterclockwise). That's called *early* timing.

Adjust the rear points on the breaker plate so the spark occurs (the points open) at the critical time for the right

**Light Is On Before
"F" Mark Is Reached
(Early Timing)**

cylinder. DO NOT move the breaker plate; leave it where you set it in timing the left cylinder. Move only the rear points to time the right cylinder.

With the rotor marks lined up, adjust the points until the test light turns on. You have to loosen the points mounting screw slightly. Notches on the point-set base let you move the points slightly with a screwdriver. Rotating the alternator rotor, the light must come on just as the marks line up.

After adjusting the rear points, recheck the timing for both sets of points. The light should turn on exactly as you turn the rotor so the marks line up. You may have to adjust back and forth between plate (front points and rear points) a few times to get both exactly right.

With Rotor Set On "F" Adjust Rear Points Gap Where The Bulb Just Lights

With Everything Tightened Recheck

Counterclockwise

Bulb Should Light Just As Marks Align

This procedure, performed correctly, contributes a lot to engine operation. It improves gas mileage considerably. Do not replace the alternator cover yet. You need it off to help you adjust valve clearance.

If you decide you need to change the condenser in this machine, raise the fuel tank out of the way. The condenser mounts just above the coil and on the same bracket.

Two Phillips screws hold the condenser. A pair of vise-grip pliers can help you loosen the screws if they're tight. Use a screwdriver to finish removing the screws. The condenser wire plugs into the wiring harness that runs to the points. Pull this wire loose and remove the old condenser. Then reverse the procedure to install the new condenser.

With every tune-up of an engine like this one, you should adjust clearance between valve stem and rocker arm. Consider this part of timing.

Unscrew the metal plugs in the rocker-arm cover. You will find one plug at the front and one at the rear of the cylinder head. There is a pair on each side, for each cylinder. Start with the valves for the left (front) cylinder.

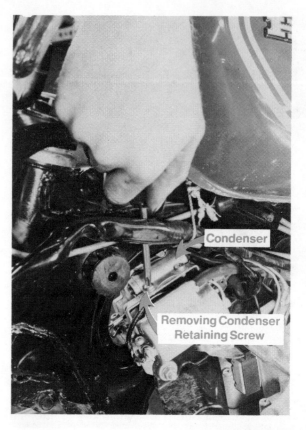

Condenser

Removing Condenser
Retaining Screw

Removing Plug In Rocker-Arm Cover

With the plugs out, turn the alternator rotor to line up the "LT" mark with the mark on the alternator pole piece. Try to wiggle the rocker arm, feeling for a tiny amount of play. If you find the rocker arm tight, twist the rotor counterclockwise one complete revolution. Again line up the "LT" mark. This puts the valves in a position to let you measure the clearance.

Line Up "LT" Mark To Measure Left Valve Clearance

For the left cylinder, locate the adjustment screws with their locknuts at each end of the breaker-plate housing. The front screw adjusts the exhaust valve, and the rear screw adjusts the intake valve.

Loosen the locknut while you hold the screw in place with a screwdriver. Select a .004-inch feeler blade to set the exhaust valves. Turn the adjustment screw until you can slide the blade between the rocker arm and the valve stem. Both rocker arm and valve stem must touch the feeler gauge lightly.

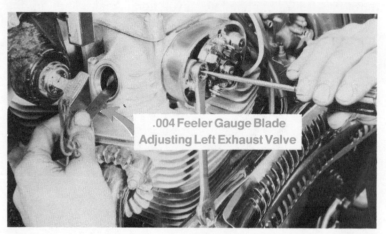

.004 Feeler Gauge Blade
Adjusting Left Exhaust Valve

There is a small mark stamped on one side of the end of the screw. The mark must point away from the breakers. Adjustment will not be right if the mark aims toward the breaker points.

Mark Should Point
Away From Points

Adjust the left intake valve. Pick a .002-inch feeler gauge. Again be sure the mark on the end of the adjustment screw points away from the breaker plate. (The screws turn an eccentric wheel inside to move the rocker arm. The wrong side of the wheel touches the rocker arm if you leave the mark oriented toward the points.)

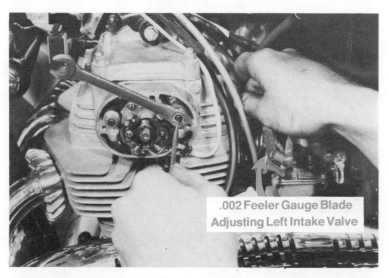

.002 Feeler Gauge Blade
Adjusting Left Intake Valve

On the right side, you'll have to remove the fuel line from the gas tank before you can adjust the right intake valve. Lift the tank up enough to provide clearance while you make the adjustment.

Adjustment screws for the right-cylinder valves are inside a housing that looks the same as the points housing. Turn the alternator rotor one full revolution, and again line up the "LT" timing mark. This situates the right-side rocker arms in position for adjusting. Set the valves, using the same procedure and clearances you did on the left side—.002-inch for intake (rear port) and .004-inch for exhaust (front port). Replace the port plugs.

Replace the alternator cover. Make sure the rubber O-rings around the cover screws stay in place. They keep oil from leaking. Set the fuel tank back where it belongs and you are all set to go riding.

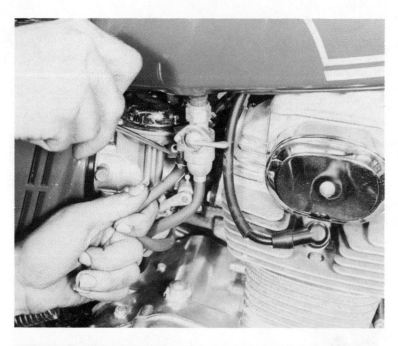

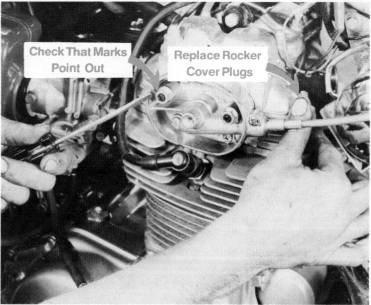

Check That Marks Point Out

Replace Rocker Cover Plugs

O-Rings Keep
Oil From Leaking

The ignition-tune-up sequence on the remaining pages of this section relates to a single-cylinder two-cycle engine. Start by changing the spark plug. Use a ratchet and spark-plug deep socket.

Set the gap between the ground and center electrodes with a feeler gauge. Your Owners Manual tells the gap for your particular motorcycle. The gap varies widely for different brands and sizes of two-cycle engine.

Breaker points and condenser mount on the lower left side of the engine. Three Phillips screws hold a cover over the alternator rotor and breaker points. Do not damage the gasket under the cover.

Rotate the alternator rotor until the points and condenser line up with the opening in the rotor. Now you can replace and/or adjust the points somewhat as on any other motorcycle engine. The points open only when the opening in the rotor uncovers them. Your Owners Manual lists the gap for your particular model.

There is very little difference in design or operation of a two-cylinder two-cycle engine. Before you remove the spark plug, notice the top of it. Some Japanese brands do

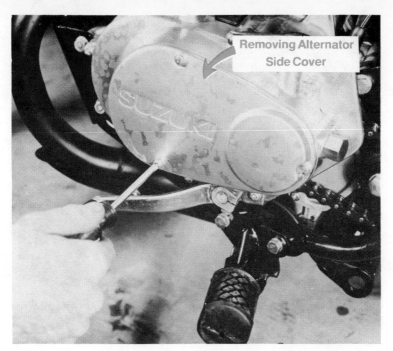

Removing Alternator Side Cover

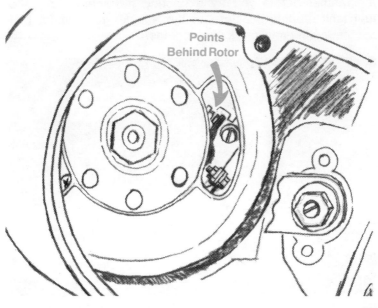

Points Behind Rotor

Adjustment Made Through Opening

not use a cap nut. A spring clip inside the spark-plug wire end grips the top threads tightly.

Loosen the spark plug with socket and ratchet. Remove the ratchet before you try extracting the spark plug. The fuel tank mounts so close to the engine, you cannot pull out the ratchet and spark plug together.

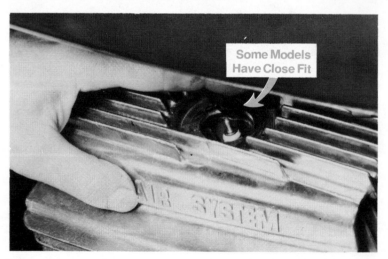
Some Models Have Close Fit

After you have loosened the spark plugs, finish removing it by hand. Check the condition. They tell you a lot about the condition of the engine and how it runs. Set the electrode gap on a new spark plug, or clean and regap the old plug.

Breaker points and condenser mount down low on the left side of the engine, behind a chromed cover. Remove all but one Phillips screws. Loosen the last screw and rotate the cover out of the way.

This model also utilizes a dual-point system. One set of points fires each cylinder. Replace both point assemblies as described for other models. Carefully set the gap on

each set of points for the spacing listed in your Owners Manual. Crank the engine and recheck the gap on each set of points, just to make sure they are spaced properly.

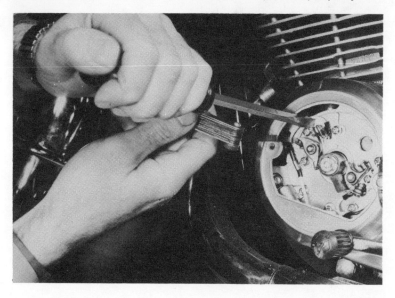

SECTION

Electric Circuits

The battery in many motorcycles mounts under the seat which protects it from weather and possible breakage. It requires monthly attention for maximum life. Corrosion around the battery terminals constitutes the worst problem. Clean the terminals and the cable ends with a wire brush. Wash the terminals and the battery case with a

baking soda solution to remove oxides formed by acid fumes from the battery.

Afterward, coat the terminals with light grease or petroleum jelly to retard corrosion. Both procedures extend the life of the battery greatly.

A rubber strap may hold a cover on the battery. Remove the strap and cover to check the water level. Remove all of the caps and look into each cell. Never assume that all cells hold fluid at the same level; they don't.

Use only distilled water or electrolyte acid to refill—never use water from a faucet. Minerals in the water cause corrosion of the lead plates inside the battery. Most motorcycle dealers and auto-supply stores carry plastic bags of electrolyte.

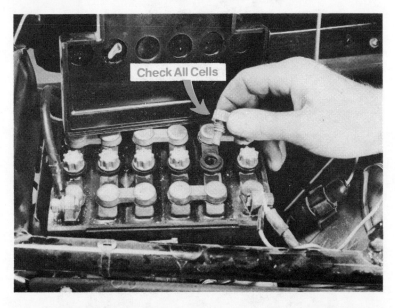

Check All Cells

Not all motorcycle batteries look the same, even though they perform the same functions in the electrical system. The battery in this model incorporates a small window in the side of the case. You check acid level simply by looking at the visible side of the battery.

To add acid or water to this battery, remove the strap clamp from the top of the battery. Remove the nut from the bolt and swing the clamp forward out of the way if you need to clean the battery.

The metal cover over the battery lifts off after you have removed the strap. This exposes the caps on the cells. Remove the caps to add electrolyte or distilled water. Always wipe off any spilled acid or water immediately. Moisture or acid on top of the battery leads to oxidation and corrosion.

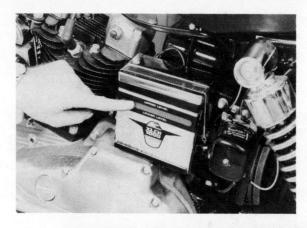

Remove Top To Clean Or Add Water

Check All Cells And Wipe Off Spilled Water

Always disconnect the ground cable from the battery terminal before you undertake any electrical repairs. This prevents arcing a hot wire against the motorcycle and burning the wire, paint, or the chrome. The arcing might also blow a fuse.

A fuse protects the electrical system on all newer street-model motorcycles. The fuseholder hides behind the left-side cover or under the seat on most models. The fuse burns out whenever something (a short or other malfunction) overloads the electrical system.

Removing Left Side Cover To Locate Fuse

A fuse sometimes vibrates apart, but that's normal for motorcycles. A short circuit blows a new fuse right away. Your dealer is equipped to find and repair a short circuit. It takes tools, equipment and experience to trace a short circuit.

In other machines, you may find the fuseholder on the fender behind the battery. Pop the fuseholder out of its mounting bracket. Twist the fuseholder to separate the halves and free the fuse. Reverse the order to install a new fuse.

Wires worn bare cause most of the short circuits on motorcycles. You can often find the worn insulation by just

91

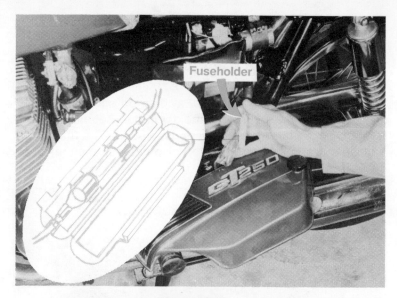

Fuseholder

Fuseholder

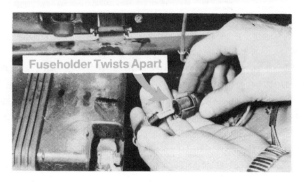

Fuseholder Twists Apart

looking carefully. If a new motorcycle burns out fuses, take it to the dealer. He will have to search out the short circuit.

To replace a burned out headlight, loosen the one screw at the bottom that tightens the ring around the bulb rim. Remove the clamp ring. Slide the bulb out of its rubber collar. Unplug the wiring from the back of the bulb.

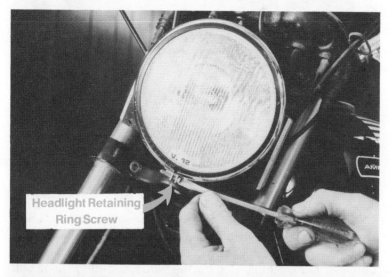

Headlight Retaining Ring Screw

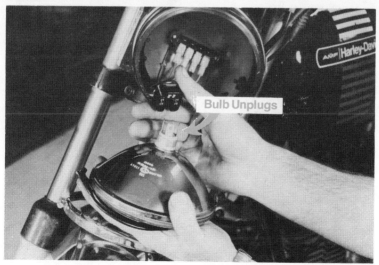

Bulb Unplugs

Push the connector onto a new bulb and replace the bulb in the housing. See that the rim of the bulb seats snugly in the groove inside the rubber ring. Hold the rubber ring away from the bulb while you slide the bulb into the headlight housing. Replace the clamp ring.

The turn-signal flasher in some machines mounts under the seat beside the fuseholder. Whenever the flasher burns out, the turn-signal lights usually burn but do not flash. To cure the fault, simply unplug the wires and plug them onto a new flasher.

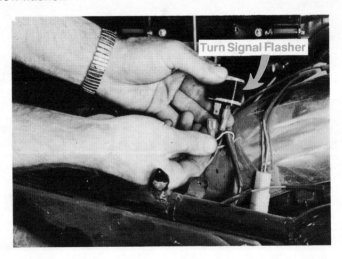

You will find the turn-signal flasher directly behind and above the headlight on this model. An aluminum plate over the headlight covers all of the wiring. The flasher attaches to the underside of this plate.

To replace, pry the flasher loose from the plate with a screwdriver. Slide the old flasher out and the new one in. Be sure the wire connections are snug on the new flasher. Then push it back into its socket with the screwdriver.

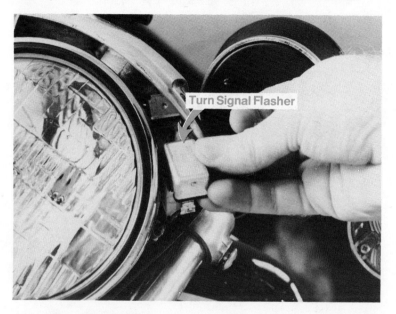

Turn Signal Flasher

A red reflector lens protects the taillight bulb from breakage. Two phillips screws hold the lens, sometimes with a metal ring. Remove these screws and the lens to expose the bulb. Now grasp the bulb, push inward on it, and twist counterclockwise. That releases the base pins, and you can pull the bulb out of the housing.

Before you try to install a new bulb, orient the pins on its base to correctly fit the socket. The pin on one side of the base is situated higher than on the other side. Slots in the socket match the staggered pins. This way you cannot install the bulb backward. Check the socket for corrosion. Clean it with sandpaper inside and out, if necessary.

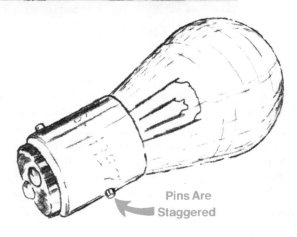

Pins Are
Staggered